Growing and Showing
Geraniums

Alan Shellard

David & Charles
Newton Abbot   London   North Pomfret (Vt)

To my fellow competitors, past and present, for their friendship and their achievements in consistently advancing the quality of pelargonium exhibits. Especially to Jack and Jim, my travelling companions, for their help, encouragement and enjoyable company.

Diagrams by Merseyside Graphics Ltd

British Library Cataloguing in Publication Data

Shellard, Alan
   Growing and showing geraniums.
   1. Geraniums   2. Flower shows
   I. Title
   635.9'33216   SB413.G35

   ISBN 0–7153–8575–5

Photoset in Souvenir by
Northern Phototypesetting Co, Bolton
and printed in Great Britain by
Redwood Burn Ltd, Trowbridge, Wilts
for David & Charles (Publishers) Limited
Brunel House   Newton Abbot   Devon

Published in the United States of America
by David & Charles Inc
North Pomfret   Vermont 05053   USA

Contents

Introduction

Most geranium exhibitors enjoy showing more than they enjoy winning. Of course we take great delight in winning but it is even more satisfying when our plants triumph in good company. Taking your plants to a show is the only way to find out if they are really as good as they look in the greenhouse, and how well they compare with other growers' plants. I have been very conscious that I might come face to face with a reader while exhibiting at some future show, so I have tried to include everything I know in the following pages, to avoid being accused of keeping something back to improve my own chances! However, this is not to say that showing geraniums is complicated and serious – as you will find out at your first show.

The geranium family is almost unlimited in its variety and the pelargonium section of that family (to which this book is devoted) is almost as diverse in its own right. Consequently, there are exceptions to every general rule of plant culture that I may suggest to you. Some of those exceptions will become the subject matter of specific advice later on – the remainder should only be associated with the idiosyncracies of individual varieties and you will discover those as you go along, by trial and error.

Those who have seen my less successful exhibits will quickly realise that the advice I give is a case of 'Do as I say and not always do as I do'. I admit to having too little time but being unable to resist growing too many plants.

I have not mentioned the enjoyment you will find amongst the friends you will acquire; this stands head and shoulders above any other reason for joining the élite and unique band of geranium exhibitors. Remember, to join, you don't have to win – just exhibit! I'm sure I can say, on behalf of all my fellow exhibitors, 'We look forward to meeting (and beating) you soon.'

1 Judging Rules and Recommended Varieties

Two exhibitors with plants of similar merit could argue all day as to which is the better. By the time we have nurtured and fussed over our plants for twelve months or more, they have become part of the family – and some people don't lightly accept criticism of their children! So competitions must have a set of rules and an impartial judge to apply them. Judges, like referees, seldom manage to satisfy everyone and it is important to understand their difficulties. They too must understand how important it is that they perform their duties with the utmost diligence and care – because in a couple of minutes they pass judgement on a plant someone has taken twelve months to prepare. Show secretaries could help here: too often they ask judges to adjudicate too many plants in too short a time, and the judge does have a secondary duty to assist in the smooth running of the show.

The fact that there are at least four different sets of judging rules that can apply to zonal, regal and ivy-leaved pelargoniums is initially daunting. However, for United Kingdom exhibitors the rules of the International Geranium Society can be ignored, and as at the time of writing the two British societies have agreed to adopt the same set of rules, only two sets of rules will apply from 1984.

The Royal Horticultural Society issues a *Show Handbook* (third revised edition, 1981). Despite the existence of the more detailed and specific rules of the British societies, most of the pelargoniums at local shows will be assessed by general horticultural (flower) judges using the pointing system laid down in the RHS *Show Handbook* and applying the definitions it contains. The RHS defines two different assessment scales – one for zonal and regal types and the other for ivy-leaved types. The specialist societies introduce further scales for more specific division of types, but we will deal with those later. For most flowers or flowering plants, the RHS uses a 20 point scale as follows.

Zonal and Regal Pelargoniums

For these, the 20 points are allocated as: 5 points to the overall plant, 5 points to the flower trusses, 3 points to the flower pips, 4 points to the flower colour and 3 points to the foliage.

Judges are advised to look out for these merits:

A shapely plant, proportionate in size to the size of the pot. Trusses should be held well clear of the foliage, proportionate in number to the size of the plant and of bright, clear and distinct colour. Large, round flowers (pips) with broad overlapping petals.

Defects are listed as:

A misshapen or partly defoliated plant with too few trusses for its size. Trusses which are small, thin or have too few fully expanded flowers (pips) or have weak stems, or stems which do not hold the flowers clear of the foliage. Leaves which are coarse, yellowing or dirty, or which show evidence of insect injury or disease.

Ivy-leaved Pelargoniums

Here the 20 points are allocated as: 8 for the overall plant, 4 for the trusses, 3 for pips, 2 for colour and 3 for foliage.

Meritorious features for ivy-leaved types are:

A floriferous plant of pleasing form. Ample, healthy, clean and bright foliage. Trusses which are fully expanded and clear of the foliage. A bright, clear and decided colour.

The defects mentioned are:

A plant which is of unpleasing form or is partly defoliated or has insufficient flowers. Coarse, yellowing, dull or dirty leaves. Trusses which are not fully developed or are not clear of the foliage.

Notice that 60 per cent of the points are allocated to flowers in the case of zonals and regals, and only 45 per cent to flowers for ivy-leaved types. This sensible variation is taken even further by specialist societies to meet the more demanding requirements of such types as ornamental-leaved zonals and species. It would hardly be appropriate to give 60 per cent of the available points to the flowers of the tricolour-leaved zonal 'Henry Cox' when it is primarily grown for the beauty of its foliage.

Here is the full text of the first 'National Rules' to be published jointly by the British & European Geranium Society and the British Pelargonium & Geranium Society; differences to the RHS rules are discussed on page 10.

The Judging of Pelargoniums (Geraniums)

The table below indicates the maximum points which may be allocated by a judge according to the various qualities of an exhibited plant(s) dependent on the general classification of that plant(s) and not on an artificial classification imposed by a schedule wording, e.g., in a class for "a zonal pelargonium" an ornamental leaved zonal will be pointed as Class 2 (below) despite the fact that all other exhibits might be pointed as for Class 1.

General Classification	Cultural Quality	Foliage	Flower Heads (Umbels)	Staging & Display
1. Zonals other than '2'	30	15	45	10
2. Ornamental leaved zonals	30	45	15	10
3. Regals, Uniques & Angels	30	15	45	10
4. Ivy-leaved other than '5'	30	15	45	10
5. Ornamental Ivy-leaved	30	30	30	10
6. 'Hybrid Ivy'	30	15	45	10
7. Scented leaved & Species	50	30	10	10

	Form & Colour	Cultural Quality	Staging & Display
Cut Blooms	60	30	10

N.B. (1) For 'groups of plants' (i.e., two or more plants or cut blooms) each plant/cut bloom will be pointed individually and up to an additional 10 points per *plant/cut bloom* allocated for uniformity as between plants/cut blooms and overall effect, i.e., a three pot class would have 330 points available (3 x 100 as per above table plus 30 for uniformity and effect).

In a two plant 'group' where 2 totally contrasting plants are exhibited both will be regarded as being non-uniform.

(2) 'Collections' and 'Displays' (i.e., plants exhibited for overall effect rather than as individual specimen plants) will have equal recognition given to (a) overall effect, (b) the apparent cultural quality of the plants and (c) the diversity of varieties included in the exhibit.

(3) It is accepted that a judge might not find it necessary to physically allocate points to all, or indeed any, plants in a particular class in order to perform his principal duty of selecting the 3 (sometimes 4) best exhibits in their order of merit. His decision, however, should always be justifiable by application of the above points table and on no other basis.

Interpretations & Definitions

"General Classification"

1. *Zonals other than Ornamental Leaved Varieties* will embrace 'basic zonals', dwarfs and miniatures (all including golden and bronze leaved varieties), genetic Hybrid Ivy-Leaved varieties which display little or no ivy-leaved characteristics i.e., 'Deacon' varieties, and 'Stellar' varieties.

N.B. In classes specifically restricted to golden and bronze leaved cultivars judges will be expected to disqualify those plants which are showing a tendency to green leaves.

2. *Ornamental Leaved Zonals* will include only those varieties having leaves of two or more distinct colours with clearly defined edges, other than the basic zone when present. (Tricolours will be those varieties on which the leaf zone overlays two or more of the other distinct leaf colours.)

3. *Regals, Uniques and Angels* will include all such types, the term 'Angel' extending to cover all small leaved regals.

4. *Ivy-Leaved other than Ornamental Ivy-Leaved* will embrace all such types including small leaved ivy-leaved varieties and genetic Hybrid Ivy-Leaved varieties which display little or no zonal characteristics.

5. *Ornamental Ivy-Leaved* will include all those types having white or cream veined leaves or having leaves of two or more distinct colours other than the basic zone.

6. *'Hybrid Ivy'* will include only those genetic Hybrid varieties which clearly display characteristics of both zonal and ivy-leaved plants without being predominantly one or the other.

7. *Scented Leaved & Species* will include all species and primary hybrids.

"Cultural Quality"

(a) *Plants* Penalties will be imposed under this section for plants displaying one or more of the following adverse features:

1) growth disproportionate to size of pot, 2) plant itself of disproportionate height or width, 3) misshapen, 4) having bare stems, 5) foliage not down to pot rim, 6) disease, 7) pests, 8) lacking in freshness, 9) unclean, 10) lack of scent (if applicable), 11) overall discolouration of foliage and 12) excessive lushness or weakness.

(b) *Cut Blooms* Penalties will be imposed as above insofar as the features can be applied to a cut bloom (see Form & Colour – N.B.) including leaves if the bloom is displayed with leaves.

N.B. (1) In this and subsequent sections (other than Uniformity & Effect in the case of 'Groups') the maximum penalty for *any one* of the adverse features mentioned should be one-third of the total points available for the section.

(2) Judges are expected to satisfy themselves that pests discovered on a plant were present on the plant prior to staging (e.g., damage or colonization) before imposing penalties.

"Foliage" Penalties will be imposed for: 1) damaged leaves, 2) deformed leaves, 3) marked or discoloured leaves, 4) sparsity of foliage, 5) excessive lushness, 6) dead leaves and 7) & 8) in the case of ornamental, golden or bronze leaved varieties, poor colours and poor definition of colours.

N.B. A judge will not penalise under this section for a fault already penalised under Cultural Quality.

"Flowerheads" Penalties will be imposed for: 1) & 2) flowerheads disproportionate to size of plant (both as regards dimensions and numerically), 3) weak stems, 4) lack of consistency, brightness &/or clearness of colour, 5) dead florets, 6) marked florets, 7) misshapen stems or heads, 8) lack of symmetry in placement

of flowerheads, 9) lack of freshness, 10) lack of following buds.

N.B. As Foliage (above).

"Display & Staging" Penalties will be imposed for: 1) dirty pots, 2) obtrusive staking, 3) lack of, poor, over-elaborate or incorrect labelling, 4) algae &/or dead matter on soil surface, 5) poor general impression.

"Form & Colour" Penalties will be imposed for: 1) poor shape, 2) smallness, 3) inconsistency of colour, 4) dullness in colour, 5) lack of freshness, 6) marked florets, 7) dead florets and 8) misplaced florets.

N.B. Judges will generally penalise under this section for adverse features which might equally be penalised under "Cultural Quality" but having done so will not further penalise when considering "Cultural Quality".

General Notes for Guidance

(a) *Plant Proportions* A plant, intended to be grown as a bush, should (insofar as the foliage is concerned) be approximately twice as broad as it is in height above soil level. Flowerheads should be clear of the foliage to give a balanced effect to the plant. It should be remembered that the plant is required to be proportionate to the size of the pot which is difficult to define although a *minimum* requirement for any well proportioned "bush" plant would be that the distance between the pot rim and the top of the foliage is no less than the diameter of the pot.

(b) *Miniature Zonals* shall be grown in a pot *not exceeding* 3½in (9cm) in diameter and the plant shall be proportionate to the size of that pot with flowers and leaves proportionate to the size of the plant.

(c) *Dwarf Zonals* shall be grown in a pot exceeding 3½in (9cm) but *not exceeding* 4½in (11½cm) in diameter and the plant shall be proportionate to the size of that pot with flowers and leaves proportionate to the size of the plant.

(d) *Basic Zonals* shall be grown in a pot exceeding 4½in (11½cm) in diameter and the plant shall be proportionate to the size of that pot with flowers and leaves proportionate to the size of the plant.

(e) *Standards* are plants grown on a straight, clear stem, the height of which stem (measured from soil level to the point of the first break) should exceed the height of the foliage above (measured from the first break to the highest point of the foliage). That part of the plant above the first break should conform to the proportions indicated in (a) above as if the first break were the level of the soil. A plant grown as a trailing standard would be acceptable even though the trailing foliage obscures the clear stem and in such cases the height of the clear stem (whether visible or not) should be a minimum of twice the diameter of the pot.

N.B. Plants which fail to comply with any of the above requirements will not be disqualified (unless in breach of the schedule wording) but will be penalised under the appropriate section, to a degree in accordance with the lack of proportion.

(f) *General*

1) *Misshapen* refers to the common failings of plants which are one-sided or badly balanced (pots not directly below the centre of the plant) as well

as uneven growth of one or more stems.

2) *Good Shape* A plant having a good shape would be one which appears to be well balanced and uniform when viewed all round, other than those trained for special effect such as a naturally trailing cultivar trained upwards on a trellis which might only be viewed with effect from two sides.

3) *Florets* (syn. Pips) are ideally large and round with broad over-lapping petals except in the case of species and the like.

4) *Age of Plants* Exhibits will not be penalised purely on the basis that they are over twelve months old but will be judged equally with all other exhibits.

5) *Size of Plant* A large well proportioned plant will only be penalised in relation to its size in comparison with a smaller but equally well proportioned plant (e.g., a large plant with two damaged leaves will be penalised to the same extent as a smaller plant with half the number of leaves, one of which is damaged). Whilst, in the event of equality, a judge would favour the larger plant, exhibitors should realise that the larger the plant the greater the difficulty in avoiding faults during cultivation and transportation.

The obvious difference between these rules and those of the RHS are that they adopt a 100 point system as it is felt that the 20 point scale provides too narrow a band, under each quality heading, for plants in close competition to be separated. 'Flower Heads' is also introduced as a single heading as the separate headings of 'Flower Head', 'Pip' and 'Colour' are both unnecessary and misleading and also carry disproportionate points relative to each other and the overall plant.

This chapter has indicated the two basic sets of 'rules'; obviously only one of them can be applied when an exhibit is judged. Despite the apparent differences, I would confidently expect a good judge to arrive at the same result irrespective of the rules or points allocation he used.

Some Recommended Exhibition Varieties

The following recommendations may enable beginners to gain a lot of experience and perhaps a little success. They are chosen because, in my experience, they are among the easiest to grow well.

Basic regals
'Aztec' (white flowers with heavy red markings)
'Hazel Harmony' (mallow-purple with deeper purple markings)
'Hazel Perfection' (soft-purple with almost black markings)

'Aztec', a regular winner in regal classes. Note the blooms covering the sides of the plant and the clear, uniform petal marking. The gap in the flowers (centre-left) is unfortunate and would result in a small loss of points, but an excellent plant despite that

Dwarf (Angel) regals
Not really an ideal type for beginners, but if you must!
'Mrs G H Smith' (white with pink-and-rose markings)

Basic green-leaved, single-flowered zonals
'Highfield's Choice' (pale lavender-pink, diploid)
'Highfield's Supreme' (cerise-red with white eye, diploid)
'Ashfield Serenade' (pale lavender-pink, tetraploid)

Basic green-leaved, double-flowered zonals
'Regina' (appleblossom-pink)
'Brenda Kitson' (pale rose-pink)
'Ashfield Monarch' (bright red)
'Highfield's Festival' (pale rose-pink, semi-double only)

11

'Henry Cox', the most colourful tricolour zonal, showing how this naturally leggy cultivar can be controlled. This plant requires a couple more weeks for the blooms to develop, and the small leaf growing among the florets of the left-hand bloom should have been removed

Gold/bronze-leaved zonals
'Jane Biggin' (strawberry-pink, double)
'Susie Q' (soft pink, single)
'Occold Embers' (two-tone pink, double with dwarf habit)

Tricolour-leaved zonals
Golden: 'Henry Cox' (salmon-pink, single), 'Mrs Strang' (vermilion, double)

Silver: 'Dolly Vardon' (vermilion, single), 'Miss Burdette Coutts' (vermilion, single)

Bicolour-leaved zonals
'Frank Headley' (dawn-pink, single). A variety in a class of its own compared to others of this type

Dwarf zonals
'Deacon Lilac Mist' (pale lilac, double)
'Morval' (blush-pink, double)
'Deacon Romance' (deep neon-pink, double)
'Ben Nevis' and 'Fantasie' (white, double)

Miniature zonals
'Tuddenham' (magenta-red, double)
'Wycombe Maid' (palest-pink flushed salmon, double)
'Claydon' (pale lilac-pink, double)
'Royal Norfolk' (rich-purple, double). Needs a lot of stopping to keep height down

Ivy-leaved
Pots: 'Sugar Baby' (rose-pink, double). Small leaves and flowers, but excellent pot plant
'Lilac Gem' (violet, double)
'L'Elegante' (white with purple-red markings, single). Excellent variegated-leaved (green and white) cultivar
Baskets: 'Red Mini Cascade' (red, single). Narrow, open petals
'L'Elegante' and 'Lilac Gem'

Hybrid ivy-leaved
Another type not really recommended for beginners; but you could try: 'Millfield Gem' (blushed white with maroon markings, double)

Cut zonal blooms and florets
Single-flowered: 'Pink Lady Harold', 'Kathleen Gamble', 'Christopher Ley', 'Princess Margaretha', 'Derek Moore'
Double-flowered: 'Duke of Buckingham', 'Ashfield Monarch', 'Regina', 'Burgenland Girl', 'Something Special', 'Sylvia Marie'

Cut regal blooms and florets
'Pink Bonanza', 'Sunrise', 'Purple Emperor', 'Hazel Stardust', 'Hazel Cherry', 'Aztec'

'Deacon Lilac Mist', a most floriferous dwarf zonal. This plant is spoilt only by the straight line of blooms at the front – a little tying or staking would have overcome this fault

'Morval', another easily grown dwarf zonal, which has golden foliage when not shaded too heavily. Minor faults here are: ageing florets in the centre of the two front-right blooms, and a gap in the centre of the plant which tying or staking could have lessened

Standards
Basic zonals: 'Deacon Jubilant' or 'Brenda Kitson'
Dwarf zonals: 'Deacon Lilac Mist' or 'Morval'
Regals and ivy-leaved: Not for beginners

Species
P. *odoratissimum* (also 'apple'-scented)
P. *graveolens* (also 'rose'-scented)

Scented-leaved
'Lady Plymouth' (variegated green-white leaves, 'rose' scent)
'Little Gem' (spicy sweet scent)

Others
'Golden Ears' (dwarf, stellar-type zonal with bronze leaves and serrated edges to the orange-red florets)
'Bird Dancer' (dwarf to basic stellar-type zonal with dark green, heavily zoned leaves. Pink flowers with narrow open petals)

You may occasionally have the opportunity to show these last two cultivars in a class for 'Stellar' types. They do meet the 'single-flowered, zonal' classification, although their chance of success in such a class will not be high unless exceptionally well grown.

Exhibitors must accept that all varieties do not acquit themselves well at shows, however appealing and attractive they are in their own right. Much disappointment can be avoided by only growing varieties that naturally possess as many as possible of these characteristics:

1 Many flowerheads (large, but proportionate to size of plant)
2 Long-lasting flowers (usually associated with a high number of florets (pips) in each flowerhead)
3 Petals that don't drop readily
4 Attractive leaves, well zoned where applicable, and of medium size
5 Pleasing flower colour
6 Short to medium length, sturdy, upright, straight flower stems

Remember that not all naturally good varieties will grow well for you, or in your particular environment. Don't persevere for more than a couple of years with a variety that doesn't appear to like you as much as you like it.

New cultivars are the lifeblood and excitement of the showbench and I would certainly advise you to join a specialist society, visit

A general view of the stock house at 'Gambles' Highfield Nurseries in Derbyshire

shows and specialist geranium nurseries and read the gardening press to keep abreast of potential exhibition cultivars. Do not buy indiscriminately. Consider the possible benefits or improvements offered by new introductions and whether they will fit into your future show plans – then make your decision.

2 Quality Control and the Show Schedule

When the BEGS rules were originally drafted they were accompanied by an additional section containing explanatory notes and recommendations, setting out the reasoning behind some of the decisions reached. These could be helpful to exhibitors. It was, for example, pointed out that while a full Classification List of all cultivars, specifying the basic characteristics of each, would be desirable, the practical difficulties of producing and maintaining it were too numerous. Exhibitors can take this as a warning not to accept blindly the descriptions in commercial catalogues. The most obvious examples are nurserymen's differences of opinion as to whether certain cultivars are dwarf or miniature zonals, and on the point where a bright pale-green leaf becomes golden-leaved. To play safe, avoid any borderline cultivars – there are plenty of others to choose from.

Awarding Points

Judges are recommended to apply the points table by assuming each plant starts with the maximum points available, then deducting points for each fault. This gives greater consistency to the marking, both between judges and between the plants appraised by one judge. Equally the notes pointed out that the severity with which a judge penalises faults should have no bearing on the final awards provided he is consistent not only towards each exhibit but also under each heading of the points table.

Judges are asked not to apply a penalty of more than one-third of the possible marks for each serious fault. This should not be misunderstood. A basic zonal, for example, exhibited without any flower at all would obviously be penalised by more than one-third (15) of the 45 points available for flowerheads. If a judge is not presented with any evidence on which to assess faults, such as the size or number of the flowerheads, then he is entitled to assume the worst and deduct 15 points for both size and number, let alone for

17

lack of consistency or freshness. Indeed, even if the plant had a mass of unopened flowerbuds, only a couple of the 45 points available could be expected.

Apart from such extremes, it is unlikely that any one isolated fault would justify a penalty of more than one-third of the points available under any one heading, and naturally not all faults are of equal importance.

Staging and Display

The 'Staging and Display' heading is only found in the Societies' points table, though the RHS does draw attention to the importance of this aspect and points out that it will influence judges. A well-presented exhibit must indeed be given preference over a badly presented exhibit – and of course good presentation has the added importance of increasing appreciation by the visiting public.

Ornamental-leaved Cultivars

The term 'ornamental-leaved' was agreed only after lengthy discussion. Previous descriptions, such as 'coloured' and 'variegated' were discarded, as it could be misleading if people argued that green is a colour and that any zoned leaf is automatically 'variegated'. The current definition admits only 'bicolour' and 'tricolour' leaved cultivars. You may come across these terms in schedules.

A 'bicolour' cultivar invariably has green and white/cream/yellow leaves, but it could have two distinct greens, provided the edges between the colours are sharp and don't blend into one another. For ivy-leaved cultivars, the second colour is extended to include leaf veins that are a different colour from the surface of the leaf. This accommodates cultivars such as 'Crocodile'. If bicolour cultivars have a zone, it should overlap one of the two colours only. If it overlays both colours the plant is a 'tricolour'. A tricolour is indeed merely a bicolour on which the zone overlays both the other leaf colours. The zone itself then takes on two distinct colours, depending on which of the other colours it is overlaying. To be a tricolour a cultivar must therefore display four distinct leaf colours. (Should it be called a 'quadricolour'?)

Golden-leaved cultivars are now excluded from the 'ornamental' definition for two reasons. Firstly, their growth habit is, almost without exception, vastly superior to bicolour- and tricolour-leaved cultivars, so that competition between them would favour golden-leaved to the virtual exclusion of the others. Secondly, modern hybridisation has produced golden-leaved cultivars of such excellent flower size and form that they should be able to compete more equally with basic green-leaved zonals than with the 'ornamentals'.

The term 'bronze-leaved' is occasionally used. This has never been defined. I have always interpreted it as applying to a golden-leaved cultivar on which the zone is so broad and pronounced that it covers the majority of the leaf surface, so giving a distinct bronze effect.

Many so-called 'golden-leaved' cultivars listed in catalogues are too near the dividing line between pale green and gold. These are best avoided for show purposes as, when grown under shaded glass, they seldom achieve the golden effect that they have when grown in the open. Indeed judges are now urged to disqualify plants which show a tendency to green leaves when shown in a class limited to gold/bronze-leaved cultivars.

Limitations on Awards

Some schedules state that 'Awards may be withheld at the discretion of the judges', which is in line with normal horticultural practice and seems to be encouraged by the RHS. The BEGS has always been strongly opposed to this practice, which allows judges to refuse to give first, second or third prizes in any particular class on the grounds that the exhibits were not of a high enough standard.

Unless schedules state that classes are 'non-competitive' then judges should not impose an undefined standard known only to them. This seems to me to be playing a game in which only the referee knows the rules. Some schedules impose limits on the number of awards allowed to exhibitors, depending on the number of exhibits, such as 'No 2nd prize will be awarded if less than 4 exhibits'. Though this is no encouragement to exhibitors to come forward, it is an acceptable precondition, provided that the 1st prize is never withheld.

Types of Pelargoniums for Exhibition

There are fourteen principal divisions or types for most exhibition purposes (as listed overleaf):

Miniature, dwarf and basic zonals not long after transferring to their final pots (*L. Craggs/Garden News*)

1, Basic zonals; 2, Dwarf zonals; 3, Miniature zonals; 4, Golden/bronze-leaved zonals; 5, Tricolour-leaved zonals; 6, Bicolour-leaved zonals; 7, 'Basic' regals; 8, Angel/dwarf regals; 9, Ivy-leaved; 10, Hybrid ivy-leaved; 11, Ornamental ivy-leaved; 12, Uniques; 13, Species and primary hybrids; 14, Scented-leaved.

Many further subdivisions could be introduced, such as single-flowered or double-flowered cultivars. Many of the divisions overlap too: there are several excellent golden-leaved (4), dwarf (2) zonal cultivars, for example. Schedule organisers are encouraged to be as specific as they can in the wording for each class, so that similar types compete with each other. Classes for more than one plant, however, are often worded so that they encourage the showing of a diversity of types.

Miniature zonals, by tradition, are not expected to exceed 5in (13cm) measured from soil level to the highest leaf. Dwarf zonals are expected to exceed 5in (13cm) but not 8in (20cm). It therefore follows that 'basic'-sized plants should exceed 8in (20cm). Failure to keep to those limits will not warrant disqualification but it will affect a judge's assessment of the plant's proportions, so it is well worth trying to stick rigidly within the height restrictions indicated.

Many cultivars, although conforming to the height requirements, have flowerheads, or florets, or leaves, that are too large or too small in relation to the size of the plant. The most common example can be frequently seen in single-flowered miniature zonals, which can have relatively massive individual florets out of all proportion to the rest of the plant. Judges are often not as harsh as they should be on these faults, but you would be best advised to avoid such cultivars, as some of us will impose maximum penalties.

The term 'standard' in a show schedule refers to the practice of training a plant to produce a long single stem and then encouraging it to produce a 'head' of stems, leaves and flowers at the top of this 'trunk'. The head should conform to the normal requirements of a 'bush' plant – as if the top of the stem were the soil level of the pot. Advice on growing these attractive plants is given on page 65 but here the definitions should be mentioned.

A *table standard* is a plant grown with a clear single stem that exceeds the height of the 'head' (excluding flowers and their stems) but does not exceed twice that height. The stem is measured from soil level to the point where the lowest branch breaks from the stem, and the head from that lowest branch to the highest part of the foliage.

A *half-standard* has a single stem, its length exceeding twice the height of the head but not exceeding three times that height.

A *full standard* has a single stem at least three times the height of the head.

The National Rules do not penalise plants purely because they are over twelve months old, and certain cultivars may in fact make better show plants in their second year (see Chapter 4). However, it must be accepted that second-year (or older) plants seldom display the freshness, vigour, leaf size and flower size of a first-year plant, which frequently results in judges correctly penalising them. Equally the advantages gained by growing a plant for more than twelve months can justify the risk – it is very much a case of knowing your cultivars sufficiently to assess which, if any, justify the longer growing period.

Judges are asked not to penalise such things as pruning scars which are not apparent from an 'external' inspection, unless of course they show ragged edges or dead wood. Even then such faults should attract far smaller penalties than any visible in an external inspection.

Size of Plants

Judges will consider a well-proportioned plant in a 5in (13cm) pot the equal of a proportionately larger plant in a larger pot, but exhibitors are well advised to take advantage of growing in a maximum pot size, if one is specified in the schedule (a good big 'un will beat a good little 'un!). However, big plants do present more difficulties in growing and transporting, so consider just how large a plant you can reasonably cope with long before you allocate a plant to its final pot.

A large plant with 3 damaged leaves out of 100 should not be penalised as severely as a smaller plant having only 20 leaves with 1 damaged. On the other hand, five times the effort is required merely to check over 100 leaves compared to 20 leaves – and therefore five times the risk of overlooking one that should be removed.

'Well proportioned' is a difficult term to define, yet once you have been around a few shows it is aesthetically obvious, a combination of a plant's width and height. Plants should also be proportionate to the size of their pot; but that does not mean that a plant in a 6in (15cm) pot should be one-fifth bigger than a similar plant in a 5in (13cm) pot. The 'proportion' of a plant to its pot depends more on the volume of the pot than on its height or diameter, so that the one in a 6in (15cm) pot may only look proportionate when it is half as big again overall as the one in a 5in (13cm) pot.

Plant proportions are generally assessed by the body (stems and leaves). The flowers are only expected to 'look right' in relation to the body. Provided the complete flowerheads are clear of, with no part below, the foliage, judges are unlikely to penalise under the flowerheads section of the points table. However, if the overall effect is displeasing, because the flowerheads are too close to, or too far away from, the foliage, then this will be penalised as a 'Cultural Quality' fault.

Although flowerheads should be clear of the foliage they do not have to be above the height of the uppermost leaves. This is important in the case of ivy-leaf and regal types, where a covering of flowers down the sides of the plant is regarded as a most desirable feature.

A good judge will consider the plant itself rather than the cultivar. Do not expect leniency because you have exhibited a plant of a cultivar that is acknowledged as difficult to grow. The challenge of

P. odoratissimum, one of the strongest (and pleasantest) of the scented-leaved species. It has no stem, but a succession of leaves from the centre of the crown, giving a well-balanced shape quite naturally. Best grown from seed with flowering stems removed regularly until 10 weeks before show date

taming a difficult cultivar is between you and your plant. Allowances will be made by judges in the case of certain species, when the plant's natural habit prevents it complying with normal accepted dimensional standards. *P. tetragonum* can hardly be expected to be wider than it is tall. However, newcomers to the showbench will almost certainly be more successful if they start by exhibiting varieties that have normal proportionate growth. Leave more unusual varieties until you have some experience.

Scent

The strength of a particular scent on a scented-leaf type is impossible to define and judges will merely satisfy themselves that such plants have a clear and distinct scent. Varieties that are both species and scented, and are shown in a class for species only, will have lighter penalties imposed for faults relating to scent than they would in a class restricted to scented-leaf types only. To do

23

otherwise would be to give the unscented species an unfair advantage.

The Show Schedule

The judging rules set out the 'quality control' requirements for show plants, whereas the show schedule should lay down clearly the actual 'specification' of the plant(s) to be shown.

An exhibitor is far more likely to be disqualified for a breach of the schedule conditions than for a poor quality plant. To have 'NAS' (Not According to Schedule) written on your exhibitor's card is a dreaded experience, if only because it means your beautiful plant has not even been given a chance to compete with the others.

Fortunately the more experienced showmen will point out any obvious errors to newcomers – most of us have wasted quarter-hours of valuable staging time searching for the owner of a plant that has obviously been placed in the wrong class on the show-bench. On the other hand old-timers can expect little sympathy.

The show-schedule wording, therefore, assumes prime importance. Newcomers to exhibiting should read any General Regulations/Rules for Exhibitors/Rules for Show in the schedule before they do anything else.

The very first thing to establish is the closing date for entries. Very few shows can risk allowing anyone, except perhaps children and juniors, to turn up on the morning of the show with their exhibits. The entry form should be completed and sent off in good time to arrive before the specified date. The bigger and more important the show, the longer the advance notice usually required.

The schedule defines exactly who may enter, which ranges from 'Open to All', for amateurs and professionals alike, to restrictive local definitions based on amateur status (perhaps made originally to prevent the village squire winning all the trophies!), residence within a fixed distance from the showground, size of garden, number of plants, whether you employ a gardener, your age and any other limitation that suits local conditions. If you are in any doubt a telephone call to the show secretary will produce a ruling.

Now you can turn your attention to the actual descriptions. Restrictions and limitations can be included very specifically within the wording for an individual class, or may be in the main rules or at some other suitable point, such as the beginning or end of a particular section. An example would be the 'Pot Plant' section of a show schedule. Under that heading it might specify: 'Unless otherwise stated, plants in this section should not be shown in pots exceeding 6in (155mm).' Under 'Class 23' you may read: 'One miniature zonal pelargonium plant – pot not to exceed 3½in (90mm).' So you are left in no doubt as to how large the plant pot should be.

The wording of individual classes depends very much on the total number of pelargonium classes available. A small local show may offer only one specific class for our favourite plant, usually 'One specimen pelargonium (geranium) plant' or 'One specimen zonal or regal pelargonium plant'. Obviously the latter wording excludes ivy-leaved, hybrid ivy-leaved, species, scented-leaved and unique types. If the former wording is used, all of these would be acceptable (in addition to regals and zonals).

Larger specialist pelargonium shows, such as the annual shows of the BEGS and BPGS, may have forty or more classes. These will include few (if any) general classes and the schedules will be worded so that like competes with like. A few classes may be slightly wider in definition, such as 'Three zonal pelargonium plants' which allows for single- or double-flowered, basic, dwarf, miniature, tri-colour or biclour varieties.

The more pelargonium classes there are, the more specific is the wording and the more limited the choice of plants eligible for any particular class. You should exhibit a plant that meets the general intention of the wording; but avoid the mistake of leaving a better plant at home, even though it falls within the definition, just because you feel it may be the odd man out. For example, in a class for 'One double-flowered zonal', don't show a badly grown basic type plant such as 'Regina' if you have a much better grown dwarf 'Morval', even though 'Morval' may be the only dwarf exhibited. If a dwarf was not acceptable the wording would have been 'One double-flowered zonal excluding dwarf (and miniature) types'.

Tricolours or bicolours could be excluded, or plants trained as a standard, or even plants having pink flowers, if the show committee wants that. Sometimes the exclusion may read '. . . excluding plants provided for in Classes 7 to 12 inclusive'. Then you have to refer to the wording used for those classes to find out which types or varieties they refer to.

There is nothing very complicated in understanding schedules, provided you pay careful attention to the wording and interpret it literally. If in doubt, ask – either fellow-exhibitors or the show secretary.

3 Growing a Show Plant: From Cutting to Final Pot

The best exhibits in a show do not arrive there by chance. They are the result of a great deal of time and hard work, some of which can be saved if you choose varieties with some of the following characteristics:

1 Self-branching habit
2 Naturally compact and bushy habit (short internodal lengths)
3 Long-lasting leaves
4 Not too thirsty and recovering well if allowed to flag
5 Sturdy, but not brittle, stems
6 Easy and quick to propagate

Stock Selection

The selection of good stock is of prime importance in producing a good show plant – even before the rooting of the initial cutting. Do not assume that because a whole plant has performed well, every stem will provide an ideal cutting. Close examination of good plants in flower can reveal that occasionally one stem is not producing a flower at every alternate leaf joint (Fig 1) – these are unsuitable. Some (particularly single-flowered zonals and ivy-leaved) carry a flowerhead at every leaf joint, usually during their first flush of flowers (Fig 2) – these are most desirable.

Tricolour zonals also frequently display one or more stems with a brighter, more attractive leaf colouring than others on the same plant. One word of warning here however; do not select stems where the chimera colour (yellow, white, etc) is excessive, as resultant plants may have a tendency to lose completely the green chlorophyll markings on some leaves and stems.

Some stems will grow too strongly, often carrying extra-large and unsightly leaves; others will appear reluctant to throw side-shoots even at the leaf joint below a flower node; some will be weak and spindly – all these should be passed over as unsuitable stock material.

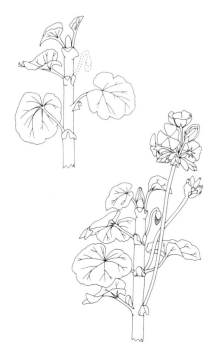

(*left*) Fig 1 A stem that has failed to produce a flowerbud. The anticipated bud is shown in broken lines

(*right*) Fig 2 A stem producing a flower at every leaf joint

'Hybrid vigour' is that elusive characteristic which gradually diminishes as varieties are continually propagated. Its loss is probably the commonest reason for once-popular varieties falling from grace. It may be impossible totally to avoid this depreciation in vigour, but you can reduce the rate at which it occurs. One of the best ways is to take selected cuttings from stock plants, about three months before you would normally take cuttings to produce show plants. If these cuttings are grown on, with a single stop, they should provide two or more healthy and vigorous cuttings just at the time you require them for next year's show plants.

'Hybrid vigour' does not apply only to a plant's apparent energy; it can affect the colour of the flowers or the extent of their double characteristic, as well as the actual size of the flowerhead or the number of pips produced in each. The day must surely come when F1 hybrids will figure amongst the cultivars that regularly succeed on the showbench, but there are none at present.

Selecting the Best Cuttings

Decide exactly how many show plants you want of each variety – it is a waste of time, space and effort to take more cuttings than you need to produce the required number of plants. Grow a few 'reserves' as insurance against the occasional rogue plant that decides to flower too early or too late or grows totally misshapen – and the potential winner that you knock off the bench!

The selection of the actual cutting is quite simple. The top three or four nodes of any stem selected as good stock should be suitable; those with the shortest internodal length are preferable.

I always try to select cuttings with a double leaf joint immediately above the node which is to become the base of the cutting. Such material usually only occurs at two stages of a plant's growth. The most common is at the leaf joint immediately above a joint that has produced both leaf and flower (Fig 3). The advantage of this type of cutting is that the resultant plant should not be shy of throwing flowerbuds.

However, the type of cutting I most favour is a 'nodal' cutting. This is a short but complete side-shoot removed from a main stem along with a small wedge-section of that stem (Fig 4). Not only are the internodal lengths invariably shorter, but quite frequently you get the bonus of extra shoots from below soil level.

The double leaf joint increases the likelihood of obtaining a side-shoot from each of the joints. These may develop at or just above compost level, and are often of equal size and vigour, so providing an ideal start towards building a well-balanced framework of branches low down on the plant.

Taking Cuttings

Cuttings removed from plants that haven't been watered for a few days seem to fare better than those taken from freshly watered plants. A little consideration for the parent plant will require you to cut the stem immediately above the leaf joint that is below the joint which is to become the base of the cutting.

Use a clean sharp knife to make the cut and trim off any jagged edges on the parent, dusting the scar with flowers of sulphur for protection. The knife (or razor) blade should ideally be sterilised after each cut by dipping in surgical spirit. A selection of blades, used in rotation, provides an obvious advantage. Remove all but the upper two or three leaves, which are retained to assist in the

(*left*) Fig 3 A normal cutting taken from the end of a stem. The shaded portion forms the final cutting for planting

(*right*) Fig 4 A nodal cutting – a side-shoot taken with a small section of the main stem. The shaded portion forms the final cutting

process of photosynthesis. Remove the stipules and finally that part of the main stem remaining below the lowest leaf joint.

Insert the cutting in the centre of a 2in (5cm) pot containing a suitable seed-type compost. Peat and sand is perhaps the most common medium, but I have successfully added, at the same time, both perlite (to keep the compost open) and vermiculite (to assist water retention) to the peat and sand.

A thin split cane will create a suitably sized hole to receive the cutting, and a pinch of powdered pumice or silver sand at the bottom of the hole seems to aid the rooting process. I also dip the base of the cutting into a vitamin C solution and then in Boots Hormone Powder, although many excellent growers scorn such mollycoddling. Experiment and make up your own mind.

Rooting

The compost can be very gently firmed toward the cutting stem, to hold it upright. Then stand the pot in water for a couple of minutes until it becomes very wet. Allow the surplus water to drain away.

Stand the pot, close to others, on a damp bed of sand or sand and gravel. If possible the cuttings should be heavily shaded for the first couple of days but after that they can receive the same light as existing plants and should not be given additional covering – maximum air movement is more important. If the bed they are standing on is kept reasonably damp, the pots may not need further watering, but if they do it is always safer to stand the pot in water.

With this method, often you need only lift the pot and examine the base to determine if the cuttings are rooted. However, it shouldn't take too long before you can tell that a cutting is rooted merely by looking at the leaves and growing point, which take on a fresher, perkier look once the roots are doing business down below.

This method of rooting cuttings should prove successful from April to October, during which period virtually all show-plant cuttings should be taken. However, if you do find it necessary to root cuttings outside that period, a heated propagating tray is most beneficial. To reduce the risk of *botrytis cineria* (grey mould), winter cuttings can be sprayed with Benlate, and the amount of water in the pot and bed reduced to lower the humidity.

Potting On

After 14 to 28 days most cuttings will have rooted and they should be moved to a larger pot as soon as rooting occurs. If you feel a cutting should have rooted, but no roots are apparent at the base of the pot, place a finger on each side of the cutting, invert the pot and tap the rim downwards on to a solid object. The pot can then be lifted off the compost and any roots can be seen.

Rooted cuttings of basic-sized plants can be potted on into a 3½in (90mm) first intermediate pot. Dwarf and miniature types should

(*top left*) Removing leaves, flowerbuds and stipules from a selected cutting. One of the leaves is being removed from a double leaf joint (*L. Craggs/Garden News*)

(*top right*) The final cut across the stem, immediately below the single leaf joint, with the double leaf joint as the following joint (*L. Craggs/Garden News*)

(*bottom left*) Dip the finished cutting into hormone rooting powder and insert into a hole in the compost (*L. Craggs/Garden News*)

(*bottom right*) Insert a plant label and place in a shaded position for a few days (*L. Craggs/Garden News*)

require only one intermediate pot – 3in (75mm) and 2½in (65mm) respectively are ideal.

Prepare your compost (see below). Use either John Innes No 1 or No 2 or your favourite soilless (peat-based) compost, and partly fill the appropriate pot. Take an empty 2in (50mm) pot, similar to the one in which the cutting is growing, and stand it on the compost so that the rim is slightly below the rim of the new pot. Trickle extra compost down the side, between the two pots, until it reaches the level of the inner pot and then give the pots one firm tap on the bench to compact the compost slightly. Top up the compost to the original level and remove the smaller pot, leaving a hole that will exactly fit the cutting with its original compost. Never try to remove a cutting (or plant) from its pot when the compost is dry. You could damage the roots, or the soil ball may crumble.

Drop the cutting and compost into the hole and tap the pot on the bench once more to settle it in. Firming is unnecessary unless the cutting itself is insecure in its original compost, in which case it may be necessary to add a little fresh compost around the stem and firm into the stem (rather than down into the pot).

If the new compost is reasonably damp (not wet), do not water it for about three days and even then do not give too much water until you are happy the cutting has settled in. Once again, give a couple of days extra shading following this operation.

Composts

While not underestimating the value of good compost, the more I learn of other growers' pet recipes, the more I realise that what matters is that you use a compost that suits you as well as the plants. Any *good* soilless or soil-based compost is suitable, but growers may gradually add more sand, grit, perlite, peat, etc, to suit their particular environment and watering habits.

Those using soilless composts, however, could consider adding extra sand (if only to provide more weight and therefore stability), and some grit to create root deviation – ensuring that the roots do not rush straight to the edge and bottom of the pot, but wander about a bit on the way. Sometimes a favoured variety that does not thrive in your usual compost can benefit from a change: in

A well-grown specimen plant of 'Frank Headley', the best bicolour zonal for show purposes. Note the profusion of blooms, and the low foliage covering the pot rim. Grown by Sarah and Dennis Shea (*W. Wilson*)

FRANK HEDLEY

particular some 'leggy' varieties are less leggy in a soil-based compost.

Ideally the pH of a geranium compost should be between 6.5 and 7.0. Anyone mixing his or her own compost from basic materials will require a base fertiliser approximating to that provided in a John Innes No 2 compost, or perhaps a little less for intermediate pots.

Growing On

From this point on, the plant must be treated as a show plant, however small and insignificant it may appear as yet. 'Timing' becomes important (see page 42) and you should have a clear impression in your mind of the plant in its various stages right up to show date. No plant is likely to conform to your picture throughout its growth, but when it begins to deviate this should ring a warning bell and you can perhaps take some remedial action to bring it back into line.

Remedial work
Stake stems that are growing in an unwanted direction into the nearest position to your ideal that they will tolerate. This cannot always be done in one operation, and you may have to pull the stem a little further towards the stake each week. Certainly the earlier in a stem's growth that you begin to correct it, the more receptive it will be. Staking early in a plant's life usually allows the stake to be removed once it has served its purpose. Twist-ties are convenient for this temporary work as they are less fiddly than twine and can easily be reused.

Sometimes you can pull a stem into position without a stake. When a gap between two stems appears too wide for subsequent side-shoots to fill adequately, the two stems can be pulled together gradually by using a twist-tie and shortening it at frequent intervals.

On occasions, you may need to rub out new shoots that are growing too close to another stem. This most often occurs when one side of the plant is carrying many more shoots than the

(*above*) A general view of the three-pot miniature zonal class at the 1983 BEGS National Show. Note the range of types available: single flowered, double flowered, green leaved and ornamental leaved (*W. Crichton*)

(*below*) A close-up of the flowerheads of the dwarf zonal 'Morval'. The petals change colour naturally as they age, but this fault seldom affects the cultivar's superiority. Plant grown by Sarah and Dennis Shea (*W. Crichton*)

opposite side, so an otherwise well-grown plant appears lop-sided. Removing shoots can also encourage new shoots to develop in a more desirable position. If a plant is allowed to develop with more stems on one side than the other, it will almost certainly finish with more flowers on that side. It is, therefore, important to create a balanced plant as early as possible in its life.

Provided you are familiar with a plant's normal growing habit you can usually correct any natural faults by early training. The two obvious examples are varieties that have a tendency to grow too upright, so that the fully grown plant lacks width; and conversely the varieties that tend to have prostrate stems, when the plant lacks height. Both of these traits can be partially overcome by early use of stakes to pull the stems of the former down and out, and of the latter up and in.

Good growing habits

The above are remedial actions to correct maverick plants. The following are normal good growing habits which contribute far more to the well-being and appearance of the final plant.

Water your plants regularly but never to excess. Preferring to water plants from the bottom, I have accumulated enough margarine tubs and larger deep-sided dishes to accommodate almost all my pots. I pour sufficient water into each dish for the plant to take up by capillary action, then within an hour return to pour away any surplus water. However, I do like to give a top watering about once a month, to wash out any harmful salts that have been carried up the pot.

If a plant has been seriously overwatered, immediately knock it out of its pot and stand the compost on folded newspapers in a shady position. The newspapers should draw off the excess water within forty-eight hours; replace them with fresh ones if they become saturated. The plant can then be returned to its pot and not watered again until almost dried out.

To give liquid fertiliser with every watering is the safest way to ensure a plant receives adequate nourishment. Adjust the strength of the fertiliser according to the frequency of your watering, to comply with the manufacturer's recommended dosage, but try to see that the plant is fed with every drink. This will considerably reduce the risk of over or under feeding.

During this pre-flowering period of a plant's life it will respond to a high-nitrogen fertiliser, to encourage strong healthy stems and leaves. Such fertilisers can be recognised by their NPK (nitrogen, phosphate and potash) ratio, given on the label. 'High nitrogen should have a higher ratio of nitrogen to the others, such as 2:1:1. I use Chempak Liquid Feed No 2, which has a 25:15:15 (approx 1½:1:1) composition, for its convenience, its trace-elements content and the fact that it has served me well for years. You too will probably settle on a favourite fertiliser.

Provided the weather is suitable, you can give an occasional light spray with clear water in the evenings. This keeps the plants perky and has the added advantage of cleaning the leaves a little. While spraying, any good systemic insecticide can be added to prevent infestation by aphids and whitefly. To spray with systemic insecticide in early March, June and September is usually sufficient. However, if these pests do invade your greenhouse, spray or fumigate immediately you spot them, with two further attacks at ten-day intervals. If you are troubled by botrytis, Benlate can be added to one of the early-season sprays as a preventative measure.

A very important habit to acquire is to turn every plant, at frequent regular intervals, so that new growth will develop evenly around the plant. A quarter-turn of the pot once a week should be adequate (keep the plant labels in each pot facing the same way as a reminder).

Maximum ventilation, subject to prevailing exterior temperatures and weather conditions, should always be your aim. A permanently running electric fan costs very little and creates air movement to assist the plants' transpiration process.

Geranium plants enjoy maximum light, but in a greenhouse they can get too much of a good thing. Keep the glass well washed down during the winter and in the early part of the year, but be ready to shade the greenhouse as soon as temperatures get too high too frequently, and certainly before the flowerbuds begin to open (page 45).

For both ventilation and shading, you can stand the pots outside once the weather is suitable, but try to protect them from the normal disasters that befall outdoor plants, particularly from being knocked over by wind, pets or children. Standing outside is very good for tricolour and golden-leaved zonals, although they probably prefer to be taken out of the greenhouse every morning and returned each evening.

Early in a plant's life remove any leaves that are growing into its centre. These leaves can deprive young shoots of valuable light, so that they do not develop properly. They also curtail the free

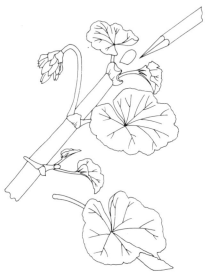

Fig 5 Using a pointed cane to remove the growing point of a zonal pelargonium. A leaf has been removed to allow a side-shoot to develop more vigorously

movement of air through the part of the plant most susceptible to rot, as well as making any rot that might occur more difficult to see. Indeed, up to four months before show date you could also safely remove any leaf, however healthy, that has a side-shoot growing from its node (Fig 5). This seems to increase the vigour of the shoot, and its leaves will grow into and fill the space left when the primary leaf was removed.

The final habit to acquire is to stop the stems at the appropriate stages of growth. This is discussed in the section on 'Timing', see page 42.

Ornamental-leaved zonals

For these, my favourites amongst all the types of pelargonium that I grow, I do vary the treatment in a couple of ways. Firstly, I feed them with a balanced fertiliser (1:1:1) throughout their life, finding that high nitrogen makes them too leggy and high potash spoils the colour balance of the leaves. A couple of cultivars with poor zone-definition may be given an occasional potash feed to darken the zone.

I also grow them 'hard' by putting them outside as often as possible, both to restrict their growth and to improve the leaf colouring. Should a plant develop leaves or stems that are chimera (lacking in the green content) or totally green, they should be removed immediately. Never exhibit a tricolour (or bicolour) with such leaves, as theoretically they make the plant 'NAS', though in practice you may only be severely penalised.

Final Pot

With basic-sized zonals, this section is equally applicable to the second intermediate pot, usually a 4½ or 5in (115 or 130mm) size. The final pot for a miniature *must not exceed* 3½in (90mm), for a dwarf 4½in (115mm) and for a basic, usually 6in (155mm).

If you do exceed the maximum sizes, your plant will probably be disqualified. The metric equivalent given is the 'official' conversion that is accepted; in all the above it is a little larger than the imperial size. Do not assume the manufacturer's stated size is correct, as several pots in circulation are slightly over-size. Check the actual size by measuring the *internal* diameter of the pot at the top; if it exceeds the larger of the imperial/metric limits, do not use it for your show plants. It is much better to grow a dwarf in a 4¼in (110mm) pot than to invite disqualification by using a 4¾in (120mm) pot.

The primary difference between this final – or second intermediate – potting and the initial one is that the balance of the plant in the pot must be considered. Do not worry if the plant shows a natural tendency to develop to the militant left or the hard right, provided the overall shape can be controlled in its (first) intermediate pot.

Before you make the hole in the compost (just as you did in the intermediate pot), identify the centre of the plant and ensure that this is as near as possible above the middle of the new pot. Invariably this means that the hole in the compost needs to be set to one side of the pot. Once you have put the compost around the new, empty pot (page 32) you can drop the existing pot and plant inside it to check that all appears balanced.

Sometimes, due to the way stems have developed, the plant is well down to soil level on one side but not on the other. This leaning can also be disguised, by sloping the hole in the new compost to compensate, bringing the lower side upwards and the higher side down towards the pot rim.

One other useful practice is to sink the plant lower into the new pot than it was in the previous pot. There are several reasons for this: a, the lower leaves are brought nearer the pot rim; b, any low stems can obtain a little support by resting on the pot rim; c, the plant gains some extra support; and d, a little space is left to 'top dress' with fresh compost on the morning of the show. *This additional compost is not normally possible with ivy-leaved types: these should either be planted higher in the pot or be topped up when planting into the final pot.*

If you have used a compost less strong than John Innes No 2 so far, move up to No 2 level now. To increase the strength above that level does not to my mind bring any improvement, but experiment with a few plants yourself.

I do not recommend changing from soilless to loam-based compost (or vice-versa) at this time; indeed I prefer to stick to one of these types from cutting to final pot. You can safely adjust the proportions of the basic constituents a little if you feel this brings an advantage.

The watering and shading routines of the initial potting-on stage apply equally once the final potting has been done.

From now on, though, 'timing' becomes more critical. See the next chapter!

4 Growing a Show Plant: Timing, Stopping and Flowerbuds

Continue to water with a high-nitrogen fertiliser until about eight weeks before show date. Then a change to high potash is required to provide a more suitable diet for the flowers. I use Chempak Liquid Feed No 4 (1:1:2), and most exhibitors have their particular favourite for this important job, some even preferring a good tomato fertiliser.

The turning, staking, ventilation, etc, are even more important now, as time for correcting any minor mishaps is running out. If an individual plant does run into difficulties, you may now do better to promote a suitable reserve, and allocate the troubled plant to a later show, or even plant it in the garden. Much precious time can be wasted on trying to persevere with a plant that isn't essential to your plans.

Once the plant begins to produce flowerbuds, you must consider when and how you will shade it. Shading has two main purposes: one is to reduce greenhouse temperature and the other is to protect the flowers, or even the foliage of some varieties. Generally, the smaller the greenhouse the higher its temperature on sunny days, and the earlier shading will be necessary. Personally I place great importance on the benefits of maximum light and so delay shading as long as I dare. I take any other action I can to reduce high temperatures, such as damping-down the greenhouse floor with water and running a permanent electric fan.

Whatever your own approach, you will find shading is essential as soon as the plants for your first show begin to give a first glimpse of colour in their earliest show blooms. Some flower colours, particularly the reds, are affected more than others by direct sunlight in a greenhouse, but none of them actually benefit.

Do not forget to shade well down the side of the greenhouse, as far as the plant pots themselves. Pots, especially plastic ones, not only absorb but retain a lot of heat, and cool roots help to keep plants fresh. If you have adopted the earlier advice of standing plants outside, this has to cease as the flowers begin to open.

Timing: A Show Plant's Calendar

Probably the most difficult part of growing plants for a specific show is to have them at their peak on show day. Weather conditions create noticeable variations from year to year, and such other factors as the locality where you live, the position of your greenhouse and its type and size, the minimum winter temperature maintained and other environmental differences, not to mention the genetic differences between apparently similar cultivars, all affect the plant's progress. Here is a 'calendar' that has served me well for many years *in my environment.* It may take you at least a year to satisfy yourself that the calendar will work for you or to determine the approximate number of days' adjustment necessary to suit your conditions. My calendar was worked out after keeping detailed records for several years. Such records are still needed for new cultivars, to establish if they differ from the norm. You too should do likewise, if you want to be really confident of your stopping dates.

It is necessary to divide the various types of geranium into three groups that can be given reasonably similar treatment.

Group 1
Double-flowered zonals (whether basic, dwarf or miniature), and most species/scented types.

Group 2
Semi-double-flowered zonals, double-flowered ivy-leaved, tetraploid single-flowered zonals and a few species/scented types.

Group 3
Regals, diploid single-flowered zonals, semi-double and single-flowered ivy-leaved and a few species/scented types.

'Diploid' and 'tetraploid' refer to the two most common chromosome counts to be found amongst zonal pelargoniums. The two types have slightly differing characteristics, the most usually apparent being the furry feel of tetraploid leaves compared to the smoother, glossier leaves of diploid varieties. Most reputable specialist nurseries will be able to advise you about any particular cultivar you are buying.

Each show requires its own calendar. Those at the beginning of June may require you to allow the plants as much as two weeks longer between the final stop and show date than those in late

August. For this example I have chosen an imaginary show on 1 July. The calendar must be plotted backwards from that date.

1 July	Show day – get up early and cut show blooms.
21 June	Remove all open florets from Group 3 plants (excluding regals) (see Fig 7).
19 June	Remove all open florets from Group 2 plants.
17 June	Remove all open florets from Group 1 plants.
13 June	Remove all open florets from regals and increase their shading.
20 May	Flowerbuds must be being trained into most suitable position by now – continue adjusting, where necessary, right up to show date.
6 May	Disbud (remove any bud appearing above the foliage) Group 3 plants.
29 April	Disbud Group 2 plants.
22 April	Disbud Group 1 plants.
8 April	Stop (remove growing point from every stem) Group 3 plants.
25 March	Stop Group 2 plants.
18 March	Stop Group 1 plants.
11 Feb	Selective stop (taller and/or stronger-growing stems only) Group 3 plants.
4 Feb	Selective stop Group 2 and Group 1 plants.
17 Dec	All plants into final pot about now.
3 Dec	Selective stop to all plants.
8 Oct	Selective stop to all plants.
13 August	Selective stop to all plants. (This may well be the first stop to a cutting since it has rooted, and it should have been in its first intermediate pot for a couple of weeks by this date.)
2 July	Take cuttings.

The most important dates in this calendar are the final stopping dates, from 18 March to 8 April, as it is these stops which should produce the optimum show of flowers on show day. Side-shoots resulting from any further stops, after these dates, will be unlikely to produce flowers in time for the show.

Equally it should be stressed that if the stop before the final stop is carried out after the recommended date, then the resulting shoots may not have developed sufficiently for the final stop to be satisfactorily accomplished. Each date acquires importance by its effect on subsequent actions.

Some excellent exhibitors will be alarmed that I should recommend as many as five stops during a plant's life. They would be right to disagree with all but the first and last, *provided that the plant*

(*left*) A young zonal, showing two stems developed after the initial stop. One stem is growing more vigorously, causing a longer internodal distance

(*right*) The stronger growing stem has been cut well back to encourage the other stem to develop, and to create breaks from low down on the cut stem. Part of the removed stem could be used as a cutting

is showing signs of breaking naturally and producing sufficient side-shoots of its own volition. There is no need to stop a plant, to make it produce side-shoots, if it is already producing them. With regals and miniature zonals, the December stop is not usually necessary, other than perhaps on an over-vigorous stem.

Stopping has two principal purposes, separate but inter-connected. Earlier stops are intended only to help develop a framework of stems, to create a balanced, well-filled plant before it is allowed to flower. The final stop, on the other hand, is an attempt to dictate artificially to the plant exactly when its flowering period is to commence. If earlier stops are carried out at any odd time of year, the plant could arrive at its final stopping date with its numerous stems each in a different stage of development. If each of these is stopped, the ratio of flowers to stems on show date will be much lower than if most stems were at the same stage of development when stopped.

To achieve this more even development of stems, beginners may need to allow the 'timing' requirement to influence the dates on which they carry out 'shaping' stops. The calendar given should enable them to do this. You could try growing a few plants to a rigid timetable, alongside some grown purely on the basis of your experience.

Ivy-leaved types can normally be stopped even more frequently, if you think this would be an advantage. The five stops will provide a reasonable plant, but you will find that, rather than merely taking out the growing point, you are actually cutting back stems to keep the shape you require.

For beginners, a good 'insurance' is to grow three plants for every one needed for show, and stagger the timing over three weeks. Incidentally, this is an ideal system to use with new cultivars.

The Flowerbud Period

As show day draws nearer each job becomes more critical and your sense of panic increases when plants seem too far advanced or to have no chance of flowering in time. There is, however, plenty of work to be done on the plants that might still make an appearance on the appointed day.

Remove any bud that is too far advanced on the date given in the calendar. By all means vary this date, by up to a week earlier, for any 'reserves' you are growing.

Once the flowerbuds begin to appear above the foliage you need to spend time positioning them. Do not rush in at the arrival of the first bud; leave it a week and even then do not try to adjust the position of buds until you have checked just below the leaves to see where the next buds are likely to pop up. Imagine where the flowerheads from all these buds will finish if you leave them to their own devices. This imaginary picture helps you spot any clusters to open up, or gaps to fill. It may not be possible to reposition a flower-bud exactly where you want it at the first attempt; you may need to pull it towards its ultimate position a little more each week. Stakes and twist-ties are, once again, a convenient way of achieving your objective – it only needs an open U-bend at each end of the tie to exert sufficient pressure. The distance between the bends can be reduced every few days. Some cultivars tend to throw their blooms out sideways, and this can be corrected by tying blooms to vertical stakes as soon as they appear.

Unless your plant has a great many flowerheads, the most important job is to select a bud that is suitable to train as the bloom in the exact centre of the plant. If you have an abundance of potential blooms, you could use a group of three to fill the centre. Once florets begin to open, you must secure netting or other suitable protection from bees and wasps over every opening in your greenhouse.

Every exhibit will need a name-card. These can be placed on the bench alongside the pot or be displayed above the plant. To do the latter, make a ½in (12mm) slit in one end of a split cane (preferably green), and slip the card into the slit (Fig 6). Insert the cane six weeks before the show (slit it first), as near the centre of the plant as possible. The cane sometimes pushes a leaf out of position, but with six weeks' grace the leaf will have settled in. Also, any stems that still need minor repositioning can usually be pulled towards the cane below the level of the foliage. Sometimes the cane cannot be used directly, but the misplaced stem can be pulled towards another stem which has been tied to the cane. The cane and a length of thickish florist's wire can even be used to push a stem outwards, rather than pull it in.

Again, that part of the cane above the leaves can be used as a firm base for one end of a twist-tie, the other being hooked around a flower stem to keep it upright or reposition it. Having fixed the position of one flower stem this way, that stem can be used as a secondary 'stake' for neighbouring blooms. These ties can remain during the journey to the show to prevent flowers shaking about.

Leaves showing signs of fading or becoming damaged or marked during the last few weeks would normally be removed immediately. However, as you near show day you have to consider the effect of such action. A single defective leaf will lose you one or two points, but sometimes its removal might cost you more – it is surprising how the departure of a single leaf can upset the balance of a plant, cause an unsightly gap or expose a length of bare stem. Any of these can create an adverse impression on a judge and lose you points on more than one basis.

It has always surprised me how co-operative leaves are. Stems and flowers are always being 'trained', but few competitors mention leaves. Given four or five weeks, much can be achieved in the repositioning of leaves, though it is time-consuming to attempt too much. Bare stems and unsightly gaps can be at least partially concealed by gently pulling the nearest leaves downwards or even sideways. This needs to be done at least once a day.

To give blooms that extra sparkle, give the plants an extra dose of fertiliser two or three weeks before show date. I use potassium phosphate (1 teaspoon to a gallon of water) which is supposed to improve the colour and size of the florets quite noticeably.

Fig 6 A variety name-card inserted in a split cane

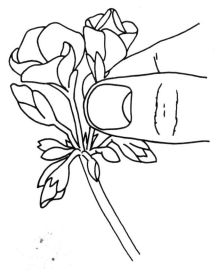

Fig 7 Removing florets from a partially developed flowerhead

Two weeks before a show all the florets have to be removed from show plants – *except regal florets, which will have been removed the previous week* (see calendar). The reason for removing all the florets is to try and ensure that no further dead or dying florets occur before the show; if they do, it is time-consuming and difficult to remove them and it can leave unsightly gaps in the flowerhead. Also, dying florets will mark or otherwise damage adjacent florets. I therefore strongly advise that all open florets are removed from the flowerhead, one at a time on the dates suggested in the calendar. Take the floret stem between finger and thumb and pull down and away from the point at which it joins the main flower stem. With a little practice, you can be confident of not damaging the following floret buds (Fig 7).

Occasionally you will find that you are leaving a mere half-dozen floret buds. On a basic zonal, this may be insufficient, although it may be just enough for a dwarf and plenty for a miniature. Only experience will help here, as each cultivar is different, but if you realise you are leaving insufficient floret buds, remove the whole flower stem to allow the plant to concentrate on the following bud.

From this point on, try to give the plant a quarter-turn daily, but if this is too much to cope with, continue with your normal weekly turning, giving the plant a full half-turn two days before the show. This completes the actual growing of a show plant, and if you have managed to do everything suggested on the appointed days, you have done very well.

Second-Year Plants

This term is used here to describe a plant that has been grown through two winters. Other growers may apply it to any plant that is over twelve months old, from the date the cutting was taken. There is an increasing acceptance that *some* varieties perform much better when grown to maturity over a longer period. What is debatable is whether such varieties are worth bothering with as exhibition plants. I think several of them are, but I prefer to grow plants steadily throughout the selected growing period, rather than to choose varieties that require to be cut back severely at the end of their first summer to provide good show plants the following year. Some respond very well to this 'cut-back' treatment – the white, double-flowered, dwarf zonal 'Fantasie' is a good example.

I am more inclined to favour February, March and April cuttings, of slower-growing or less compact varieties, grown through for the

(left) P. *graveolens*, a scented-leaved species, very tolerant to shaping by frequent stopping. This is a second-year plant beginning to develop new compact growth in early spring after being cut back the previous September (*L. Craggs/Garden News*)

(right) 'Lady Plymouth', a bicolour, scented-leaved variety similar in habit to P. *graveolens*, to which it is almost certainly related. In full bloom its apparently insignificant flowers are very attractive

following year's show. This is particularly convenient with tricolour zonals, whose cuttings seem to root well, without bottom heat, from February onwards. I seldom let such plants flower during the first summer, keeping them stopped regularly (often relying on the appearance of a flowerbud to remind me to stop the growth).

Almost without exception, I find that species and scented-leaved types make much better show plants if grown for at least sixteen months, and many certainly reward you if given six months longer than that. Species grow true from their own seed and this is an excellent method of producing good vigorous show plants that respond well to stopping, by producing an abundance of side-shoots that can seldom be achieved with vegetative cuttings.

If species or scented-leaved types bush out naturally when subjected to normal training, then they should be grown that way. Many varieties, however, do not and these should not be un-reasonably forced to conform but allowed to develop their own characteristics and merely kept tidy and within bounds.

5 The Show Itself

'Show day' really begins as early as possible on the day *before* the plant is to be exhibited and judged. If you are going to be away from home on that day, get up early enough to water all potential show plants (including reserves) before you depart. This is one of the very few occasions when plants that aren't quite ready for watering should be given a little, just to tide them over the next thirty-six hours, as you don't really want to water them immediately before the show.

You may have the choice of staging your plants during the evening before the show, throughout the night or only on the morning of the show. Large two or three day shows may allow you even longer. For shows in my own locality I prefer to stage my plants as early as the rules allow, which often clashes with another preference – to prepare my plants as far as I can before I load them up to transport them to the show. If a show is a long distance away, I aim to arrive as early as possible on the actual morning, having prepared and loaded the evening before.

Preparing plants should always be done with a copy of the schedule in front of you. Work your way through the classes you have entered, taking each plant in turn and fussing over it until you have it as near perfect as you can make it.

If you have two plants that you could use for the same class, stand them side by side and carefully select the better one. Try 'pointing' them yourself if in doubt.

(*above*) The author's single-flowered zonal 'Katrina' prepared for transport to a show. The temporary stakes prevent larger blooms waving about – and are removed on arrival at the show (*Author*)

(*below*) A compact example of the scented-leaved 'Little Gem'. Its small individual florets last only a few days, so dead and dying florets require continual removal. Grown by Roy and Joan Hinchliffe (*W. Crichton*)

LITTLE GEM

Preparation Before Loading

Top up the plant pot with a thin layer of fresh, slightly damp compost, taking care not to damage the lower leaves (if they are right down to the pot rim, lift them gently with the back of your hand).

Remove any suspect leaves, if it can be done safely, and do check the centre of the plant.

While looking into the centre of the plant (ideally from pot-rim level), use a pair of tweezers to remove any dead or dying stipules you can find on the stems. Use a ¼in (6mm) brush to remove any compost (or cobwebs!) clinging to the stems.

Closely examine each flowerhead. If any florets are dying, remove them by gripping the floret stem with tweezers *from underneath the bloom* and gently pulling it down and out. If this leaves a gap in the bloom, when viewed from above, it can often be partially concealed by carefully pulling or pushing the stems of nearby florets towards the gap – use the tweezers from below the flowerhead again. Ideally this job should be done each evening for three or four days before the show, especially if you have forgotten to remove all the florets as suggested in the 'calendar', or in a sustained hot, dry spell.

Look at the flowerheads and try to reposition any that are too close to each other, or are badly placed, or not directly above the foliage. Temporarily 'tie' blooms that might wave about in transit to a centre cane, an extra cane, or to other blooms.

Use the brush (or a slightly larger one) to remove any fallen pollen, dust, dirt or compost from the surface of the leaves.

Remove the plant label from the pot, or push it right down below the pot rim. A prominent label can spoil the effect of an exhibit, especially of a miniature.

Wipe the pot with a damp cloth to remove dirty marks.

Write the name of your chosen variety against its class on the schedule; plus a reminder of any last-minute jobs necessary when actually staging, such as removing a prominent stake that is safer left in position during your journey.

(*above*) An excellent young plant of the dwarf ivy-leaved 'Sugar Baby'. The name-card is fixed to a cane, which could also be used to position wayward stems. Grown by Roy and Joan Hinchliffe (*Author*)

(*below*) The tricolour-zonal 'Filigree' – perhaps a perfectly shaped specimen. Though this cultivar has few blooms and the zone is rather subdued on the cream section of the leaves, it still won a first prize for Ken Lea. Leaves of 'Henry Cox' can be seen on the left, and 'Mrs Strang' on the right (*W. Crichton*)

Transporting

The exhibitor who lives a few yards from the show, or one with a large (enough) van, is now at a distinct advantage, though I have seen plants brought by pram and wheelbarrow, in a wicker cage on public transport, in vans with custom-made fittings and in purpose-built trailers towed behind both bicycles and big cars.

When packing your plants, you can either space them well apart so that they hardly interfere with each other, or pack them closely together to support each other. If pushed for space I tend to favour the spaced method for my better plants and those that aren't really suitable for togetherness, such as ivy-leaved plants or regals with blooms coming down the side of the plants. The remainder I pack closely to fill the remaining space, usually including a couple of reserves if there is room. A few useful do's and don'ts are:

Do try and provide maximum support as high up the pot as possible, to prevent the plant falling over.

Do try to position plants of the same size next to each other for support.

If you are putting two or more plants in the same box, do pack newspapers in the spaces between pots to prevent them sliding about.

Don't place tall or wide plants where blooms or stems will be amputated when you finally slam the lid or door.

Do keep the distance between greenhouse and transport to an absolute minimum.

Don't carry too many plants to the vehicle at the same time; one at a time is ideal.

If you are travelling to a show early in the morning, do try and complete the loading the evening before.

My last job before leaving home is to select and pack any cut blooms (with leaves, florets, etc).

Do take your spouse or a friend along to the show – for help and encouragement.

Don't stage through the night – it is not as easy as it sounds, though a long journey, many plants and early judging may leave little option.

Show Equipment and Accessories

Any time left after loading can be usefully spent making out clear, neat name-cards for your plants. Plain white cards about 3 x 1½in (76 x 38mm) are large enough and can often be trimmed smaller with scissors, especially when used with miniatures. I use a small stencil set with pen and india ink, which produces a very acceptable appearance without being flashy.

The items that you may need when you get to a show are: show schedule; pair of long, thin scissors; secateurs; tweezers; sharp knife; safety razor blade; ¼in (6mm) brush; damp cloth in polythene bag; dry polishing-cloth; watering can; spare split canes; twist-ties; green twine; spare pots of various sizes; blocks of wood in various thicknesses, approximately 5in (130mm) square; florist's wires; cards for plant names; watch; 'bikini' type vases (if you are showing cut blooms); boards for displaying florets and leaves (if necessary); case or box in which to carry as many of these as possible.

At the Show

Before you unload any plants have a stroll around to familiarise yourself with the layout of classes. The following routine, from this point onwards, should serve you well, although you may prefer to change the order slightly and cut down on some jobs if time is short.

Collect your exhibitor's cards from the show secretary's office or table, check them against your schedule and consult the secretary about any discrepancies. If you have omitted to enter a class for which you had a really good plant, do consider whether you can enter it in another class.

Check your watch now (and at frequent intervals). You should aim to finish ten to fifteen minutes before the show area is cleared for judging.

Bring your plants into the show – one at a time is best. Hold the pot in two hands and keep it upright so that the blooms don't fall to one side of the plant. If you are a beginner, advertise the fact immediately by asking a couple of naïve but reasonably sensible questions of one or two other competitors; unless you are very unlucky (or they are in serious time trouble) they will keep an eye on you from then on, and may even pass an occasional word of encouragement about your better plants.

Get all your exhibits into the show and placed on the bench initially, without fussing over them (keep your schedule to hand). Try to secure the most central position within any particular class. If you have arrived late, you may be forced to stage towards the edges of the class or, even worse, behind other plants.

If you notice that one or two plants need a little water, give it to them immediately, *before* you put them on the bench; nothing looks worse than a plant standing in a pool of water or damp patch on the showbench.

Having got all your exhibits into the right classes, place your exhibitor's card alongside each. Not only is this a double check that you have the right exhibit in the right class, but if stewards need to move your plant they will be able to identify you and call you over. Stewards, essential to the smooth running of a show, often have to make unpopular decisions, but do accept the principle of 'first come, best position'. When classes exceed the size expected, they may have to move exhibits closer together or even move them to a different location in the show. A good steward will always announce in a loud voice that he is going to move plants and invite exhibitors involved in that class to assist. It is best to do so, or your best plant might be moved to a back corner; and you are unlikely to be allowed to change all the plants around again.

Remember the all-important unwritten rule that you must not touch another exhibitor's plant. If someone's plant needs to be moved, even by an inch, for you to stage yours, ask the steward (or the owner) to do it for you. If you have to stage your plant behind others and there is a risk of damaging them when reaching over, ask for them to be lifted down so that you can stage yours. Don't expect any sympathy from other exhibitors or stewards if the only space left for you to stage a plant is behind a bigger one that will virtually obscure yours. Stewards may rearrange plants according to size after judging, for the benefit of the visiting public, but this should never be done before the judges have made their awards.

Final 'Dressing' of Exhibits

Start the final 'dressing' of plants by stages, essential jobs first, so that if time runs out all the exhibits are at least fit to be judged. Each job should be carried out on every exhibit before moving on to the next job.

1 If you have entered the cut bloom, florets or ornamental leaves classes, stage these reasonably well (without being too fussy) and lay out the variety name-cards.

2 Take all the travelling ties and stakes off each plant in turn and decide if the variety name-cards will be best in a central stake or laid on the showbench alongside the pot.

3 Check the notes you have made on your schedule and do the important last-minute jobs you noted.

4 Visit each plant to remove or conceal any florets or leaves damaged in transit. Good first impressions will not fool a judge but they will ensure he doesn't dismiss your plant lightly. This is why a central, front position on the bench is so desirable and why, at this stage, you should try to establish which side of your exhibit looks best and make sure it faces the front of the bench. To help you find the best side quickly: try placing the plant so that the tallest bloom is at centre back; keep the barest stems to the rear of the plant – also any gaps in foliage or flowers; and try to ensure the best-positioned blooms are front, centre. Judges are unlikely to inspect every plant closely (they seldom have sufficient time). They usually dismiss a proportion of the plants as having no chance and then decide which of the remainder appear likely winners and deserve closer examination.

5 Identify the plants whose chances you can improve most with a little extra attention. Check these, to see if you have overlooked any dying or damaged leaves, florets, stipules, etc, and remove them with tweezers or scissors. Consider if a concealed stake could improve the appearance and if so, cut one to the required length with your secateurs. Use concealed twist-ties, twine or florist's wire for less severe repositioning. Remove dead wood or unsightly scars that you missed at home with a razor blade or knife. Tidy up the top surface of the compost, brush any compost, etc, off the stems, and then clean the brush and brush the leaves free of any pollen.

6 Then repeat the above with any plants you decided initially were clear winners – hopefully it is from these that you are most likely to be awarded a trophy.

7 Then give a less critical going over to the exhibits you have decided are just making up the numbers – it is surprising how often you can squeeze a third prize from these just by making sure there are no unnecessary glaring faults.

8 Stop these jobs when you have about half an hour left. At this point visit every one of your exhibits in rotation to give the pot a wipe with a polishing duster, or with a damp cloth if it has become marked and dirty. At the same time stand back from the bench to consider if your plant is best displayed as it is, or whether it would look better raised on one or more of the blocks of wood you have brought, or on an upturned pot – particularly important in multiple-pot classes, or when your plant has to stand behind a larger one. If your plant has an unfortunate gap or bare stems, it can be a positive advantage to be on the back row (see page 62).

9 If you have any time left you can catch up on any jobs you rushed over or left out. Try to be around the showbenches for the ten minutes before exhibitors have to leave, as this is the time when stewards may have to make hurried, last-minute adjustments to plant positions.

After Judging

The measure of your success will be in the number of red (1st), blue (2nd) and yellow (3rd) prize cards that you have accumulated. As a bonus, you may have been awarded additional silver or gold certificate cards to indicate your plant is of special merit and, if you have done really well, a trophy for the best this, or that, depending on the size of the show and the number of trophies. The highest honour is a trophy for 'The Best Exhibit (or Plant) in the Show', and if you are ever called upon to receive that trophy it is a moment to savour. Other apparently prestigious awards such as 'most points' or 'most prize money' in the show are not nearly as satisfying as those for 'best' of something, as they tend to indicate only a good all-round ability and the fact that you brought a lot of plants to the show. They give some sense of achievement for twelve months of endeavour, however, and prove that you have done your bit to make the overall show a success.

If you do not understand why a certain plant won and yours didn't, ask a judge; they should remain in attendance for at least an hour after judging. Much can be learned from such discussions. Every schedule has provision for exhibitors to object to judges' decisions, but you would almost certainly regret making an official objection on matters other than breach of schedule wording.

Loading up again for the return home is the saddest part of the day. Although generally it is bad practice to attempt to show the same plant at two shows, it is sometimes possible with species, and even occasionally with other types. Treat plants that have such possibilities with great care, staking and tying if necessary. The remainder can be bundled in close together without inflicting much damage. Tidy the plants and return them to the greenhouse as soon as possible. If you have future show plants in the greenhouse, plant the 'returning heroes' in the garden, so that those still to be shown have plenty of space.

The return from a show is a good time to identify good stock for future cuttings, not forgetting that the cuttings for next year's show should be taken the day after you return from this year's.

6 Less Usual Show Classes

Some shows, particularly the more specialist pelargonium shows, have classes for multiple-pot exhibits, for cut blooms, individual groups of florets, plants trained as standards, hanging baskets and even for groups of leaves. Each of these enjoyable variations deserves a few words in its own right.

Multiple-pot Exhibits

These classes usually call for between two and five pots of plants, and it pays to consider carefully the actual wording used in the schedule. If the wording states 'distinct cultivars' (or 'distinct varieties'), then the exhibit must not contain more than one of any individual variety. If that qualification is missing in the wording, you may safely assume that two (or more) plants of the same variety can be included in your exhibit.

If the class calls for 'distinct cultivars', or you intend anyway to exhibit two or more different varieties, do select plants that have a similar growing habit and type of flower. Don't try to stage a tall leggy plant with two compact ones, nor a double-flowered variety with two single-flowered ones – at least not if you have a choice. 'Uniformity' has a wide interpretation and is a criterion on which judges place high importance. If the class wording calls for a variety of types to be exhibited together, such as one ivy-leaved, one zonal and one regal, uniformity is of course less obvious, although it is advisable to select plants that are in similar-size (and colour) pots, unless a miniature or a dwarf are included in the types required.

When staging multiple-pot classes you should try to use a little artistry and a lot of thought. Fig 8 shows various arrangements. The better plants should always be given prominence, unless an unfortunate colour combination makes this undesirable. Three-pot classes should only be staged as in (b) if there is no room for (c) or (d). Plants behind others are raised up (if necessary) to give a tiered effect.

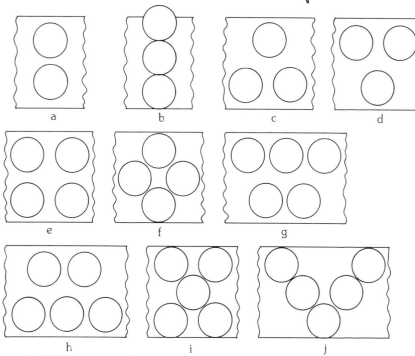

Fig 8 Various ways of displaying multiple-pot exhibits, to obtain the best effect from the plants available

Displays

Classes calling for 'displays' are the ultimate in multiple-pot exhibits, but are less popular today. If you are growing specifically for such a class, you may find it preferable to grow at least some of the plants 'one-sided'. Judges never disturb a display to examine individual plants, and the weight of flowers and foliage can be concentrated towards the front of the display if plants are grown that way.

You will have noticed from the judging rules that three equal considerations are applied by judges – the overall effect, the diversity of varieties and the apparent cultural quality. The 'overall effect' is the artistic impression, viewed from the front only. For 'diversity', the more types and varieties you can include the better; and 'apparent cultural quality' is self-explanatory. Most schedule wordings give the dimensions that the display *must stay within, including leaves and flowers.*

Ideally pots should not be apparent in a display class, and the most common method of concealment is to drape black velvet (black polythene will suffice) down the sides and around the front and hope that the foliage will cover the inner pots. You could build a stand with back and sides and even window-box type shelves (to increase the height) which will conceal the pots; if some are still obvious you can fill the base with damp peat and bury the pots in it.

Cut Blooms

These classes are popular and closely contested at many shows. They normally require one or three cut blooms, 'each staged with two own leaves in separate vases', and can be for zonal or regal types. Invest in the appropriate number of 'bikini' type exhibitors' vases, as judges tend to frown upon blooms staged in jam jars, milk bottles and paper cups.

Once again multiple classes should be 'uniform', and don't forget to watch out for the 'distinct cultivar' qualification. The normal method of staging zonal blooms is to fill the vase with wet sand, insert two leaves taken from a plant of the same variety ('own leaves') so they are reasonably horizontal, one on each side of the vase, and push the bloom in centrally above them, having trimmed the stem to the appropriate length. One bloom and two leaves only in each vase ('separate vases') (Fig 9).

Single-flowered zonal blooms are more traditionally ideal; they have larger individual florets, and therefore larger blooms, on the more suitable varieties. However, they travel badly and double-flowered varieties probably win the majority of these classes nowadays.

Regal blooms can be staged the same way, but some exhibitors retain the two smaller leaves – often found immediately below the flowerhead. In this case only the single stem need be inserted centrally into the vase until the leaves rest on the rim.

The aim of a grower entering a cut-bloom class should be maximum size without coarseness. I suspect that the majority of exhibits are blooms from 'reserve' plants that didn't make the showbench, but if you really want to explore the possibilities of these classes you should grow specifically for them. The best cut blooms are not necessarily found on the varieties that produce the best show plants, and you should extend your horizons a little when selecting varieties to grow. You don't have to build up a good plant, and cuttings can, therefore, be taken in late February (for the 1 July show used as an example in our calendar). Take side-shoots, about 3in (76mm) long. As soon as they are rooted, move them into a

Fig 9 An exhibition bloom, with leaves, in a vase. Also, various ways of raising exhibits

3½in (9cm) pot for six weeks and then into their final 5in (13cm) pot to keep them growing vigorously.

Use a stake to keep the stem vertical, and as soon as the pair of leaves above the bloom have developed sufficiently, remove the growing point between them and any side-shoots that appear. All the plant's energy is then concentrated on the bloom, with any surplus running on to the top two leaves to prevent distortion and coarseness of the bloom. I have not found regal blooms as suitable as zonals for such individual attention, but the first bloom from young, over-potted plants is usually better than most.

Do not try to transport the blooms to a show in their vases. The best method is in narrow-necked bottles (small mixer-drink bottles are ideal) three-quarters filled with water. If the stem is long enough to rest on the bottom and still hold the bloom clear of the neck this is excellent, but in any event use a twist-tie to hold the bloom firmly in position. The bottles can then be securely packed in a box large enough to keep the blooms apart. Always take a reserve bloom with you.

Florets and Leaves

If you are entering classes for individual florets or leaves you will need to prepare beforehand, as the wording invariably calls for them to be 'displayed on a board'. The maximum permissible size of board is usually stated, and is usually larger than you will require; identical-sized florets or leaves look larger if staged close together than if widely spaced, so don't use a larger board than you need – aim for a ½in (12mm) to 1in (25mm) gap between florets or leaves.

Unless the schedule requires something different, a deep matt black is the best background colour – black velvet is better than paint. Ideally, the top of the board should slope slightly forward but it doesn't need to be more than 1in (25mm) higher at the back than the front (Fig 10). Both leaves and florets are best staged by making holes, at appropriate distances apart, in the top of the board, through which the stems can be easily inserted.

With any luck your reserve cut blooms will provide some excellent-sized florets, and reserve show plants should provide the remainder. Good single zonal florets are much more impressive than doubles, having a more perfect 'form', which better judges appreciate in these classes. Choose a newly opened floret where the pollen is still fresh; the golden centre is a real eye-catcher.

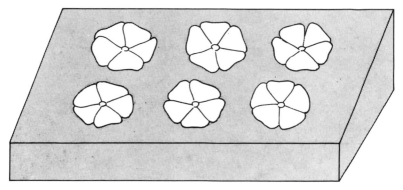

Fig 10 A typical display board. These are usually finished off by adding front and side sections to angle the florets (or leaves) towards the viewer

Ideal regal florets are not so simply described, but don't include a floret with seven petals if the remainder only have five. Uniformity of size and shape, and a good blend and balance of colours go a long way to making these exhibits effective.

The same criteria apply to ornamental leaves, although it is usually harder to achieve uniformity of size. Unfortunately, silver tricolours seldom grow to the same size as golden tricolours; it is therefore preferable to stick to one type only if you can. Although older leaves tend to be larger, their colours may be fading; while young leaves with the brightest colours may be too small. A compromise between size and colour is usually inevitable.

Don't forget that golden/bronze leaves are not classed as 'ornamental' and should not be included in such an exhibit, any more than an ornamental ivy-leaf should be, if the class wording specifies 'zonal' (as it usually does). You risk disqualification if the wording states 'named varieties/cultivars' and you omit to place variety name-cards on your exhibit. If your entry includes a floret or leaf from a seedling, you must state 'unnamed seedling' on the card; better than inserting 'Joe Bloggs', just to conform to the schedule wording. However, I am sure that 'name unknown' would avoid disqualification in a class for 'named varieties' – it would be safer not to include such a leaf or floret in your exhibit.

Transporting these exhibits to a show is relatively simple if you select them at the same time as the cut blooms and lay them on lightly dampened cottonwool covering the base of a suitable-sized tin or box. If you wish to put a lid over them a few ventilation holes are advisable, especially for a long journey.

The 'head' of a table standard of the popular zonal 'Regina'. The rather haphazard positioning of the blooms might have been improved by tying (bloom to bloom) but is made more difficult because individual stakes cannot be used

Standard Plants

Virtually any type (but not all varieties) of pelargonium can be trained as a standard. Zonals and species are the most common but occasionally a regal or ivy-leaved type will appear with its proud (and why shouldn't he be?) owner. In fact any exhibitor who can produce a good standard plant on show day is entitled to feel pleased with himself, as the growing of a standard requires special techniques and great patience. Select a variety that produces a compact plant when grown as a 'bush', rather than one that will produce a long stem quickly. The characteristics that produce such a stem are not those you require to form a good head.

Cuttings need not be as short as normal. The time of year to take the cutting is something of a lottery as it depends on the height of stem you hope to achieve. In view of transport difficulties you should aim for a 'table' or 'half' standard for show purposes and, from your knowledge of the variety you have chosen, estimate the time required for the stem to reach the desired height by the following 1 February.

Grow the plants in a larger pot than you would use for a 'bush' plant of the same age – this encourages strong vigorous growth of the stem. Don't forget to turn the plant weekly and try not to let it dry out.

Tie the stem to an upright cane from the moment the cutting is transferred to its first pot. Loosen earlier ties at frequent intervals to prevent the girth of the stem being restricted. This is a weekly job if you are to obtain the perfectly straight stem needed.

Remove any side-shoots as soon as they appear, but allow leaves to develop and die back naturally.

A couple of flowerheads can be allowed to develop, but watch that the stem doesn't grow away at an angle from the flowerhead.

By 1 February your stem should have reached the required height, and – at that time of year – should have short internodal lengths. This is the ideal time to remove the growing point, so that side-shoots will develop from the top three or four nodes (any below that should be rubbed out as soon as they appear). Remember that it is the distance from the compost to the lowest branch that determines the length of 'the clear stem', which will in turn relate to the height of the final 'head' and so determine whether you have a 'table' or 'half' standard (see page 21).

Although you might achieve a reasonable flowering 'head' by August that year, I recommend that you don't allow the flowers to develop but keep stopping the branches as they reach 2–3in (50–75mm) in length, so building up a compact framework of branches for a show plant the following year. From this point onwards the head of the plant can be treated as if it were a normal 'bush' plant.

Ensure that the final cane extends well into the 'head', both for basic support and for use in training stems into ideal positions.

Transporting standards to shows can be a problem, even if you have facilities for keeping them upright. The stem immediately below the head is a breaking-point if these top-heavy plants begin to sway about. Standards must be firmly based, to prevent the pot moving, and given additional support (diagonal ties across the vehicle are ideal) as high up the stem as possible, to prevent swaying. If you can't transport them upright the same considerations apply, but the diagonal ties also have to serve as a cradle to enable the plant to travel at an angle. Take the same care for the return journey as, with a severe cut-back each September, standards can serve you well for two or three years.

Hanging Baskets

Many shows have a class for hanging baskets, usually specifying 'ivy-leaved types'. For show purposes a 10in (250mm) basket is usually large enough, although you run the risk of being well and truly dwarfed by a 12in (300mm) basket from a local exhibitor.

A hanging basket is intended to be viewed at head height or above, so the plants should trail downwards below the base of the basket, ideally concealing it. In a 10in (250mm) basket four plants grown specifically for the purpose are usually sufficient.

I prefer to grow the plants in 3½in (90mm) dwarf pots until they are well established. One of the four plants should be turned and stopped regularly, but the other three should not be turned and, after the initial stop, need not be stopped as frequently. By December these plants can be put into the basket. The three that have not been turned should already be 'one-sided' and trailing over the edge of their pots. They can be inserted at the edge of the basket between the suspension chains. The remaining plant should be compact and bushy and will fit neatly into the centre of the basket. Weekly turning is then essential for even growth.

Baskets tend to dry out quicker than pots and will require more frequent water in warm weather. Form a hollow in the centre or around the centre plant to prevent drying out. Some modern plastic baskets have an integral tray underneath, but don't let the tray remain filled with water once the compost is saturated.

Keep the trailing branches at even lengths by stopping the longer ones. This is usually sufficient to fill out the plants so that the leaves hide the basket. I have seen stronger-growing cultivars with light weights hung from stems to pull them down, and even stems on opposite sides of the basket pulled towards each other with twine passing underneath the basket, to create a more 'balled' effect. Continue to stop the central plant more frequently – failure to do so deprives the top of the basket of flowers.

Transport is not as difficult as for standards but does require care and often a spare pair of hands. Baskets also need a great deal of space and are often best loaded up first. A sturdy bucket filled with wet sand usually provides a solid base on which to sit a basket, but make sure the bucket cannot slide about. Ideally someone should lower the basket on to the bucket while you lie down alongside, moving any trailing stems that may become trapped and making sure the basket seats centrally into the top of the bucket. Remember to take corners gently on your way to the show!

Index